NEXT

STEPS ON YOUR SPIRITUAL JOURNEY

TOMMY "URBAN D." KYLLONEN

FOREWORD BY MONTELL JORDAN

Tranzlation Leadership
TAMPA, FLORIDA

Tranzlation Leadership
1235 E. Fowler Ave. Tampa, Florida 33612
© 2019 by Tommy Kyllonen

Unless otherwise indicated, all scripture quotations are taken from the Holy Bible, New Living Translation, copyright © 1996, 2004, 2015 by Tyndale House Foundation. Used by permission of Tyndale House Publishers, Inc. Carol Stream, Illinois 60188. All rights reserved.

Cover + Interior Design: Edward "SPE©" Bayonet / iAMbayo.net

Photography: Crossover Church Social Media Team

The Next Book is available in Print, Digital and Audio formats.

ISBN: 978-1-7327782-3-8 (print)

ISBN: 978-1-7327782-4-5 (digital)

ISBN: 978-1-7327782-5-2 (audio)

Printed in the United States of America

www.urband.org

This book is dedicated to my Crossover Church family in Tampa and Atlanta. We are committed to reaching the lost, the last and the least. When you go after the ones that nobody wants, with God's help you will soon have the ones that everyone wants. God has used our church to impact people all over the world with the Gospel due to our unique, creative approach. Crossover exists to help people Discover, Develop and Display Jesus Christ in every area of their lives. We are always pushing past our comfort to help people take their **NEXT** steps on their spiritual journey.

TABLE OF CONTENTS

THIS IS HOW I DID IT... MY STORY
- Montell Jordan

I was the worst of the worst. Now, please allow me to qualify that statement—because it's simply an indictment of my inaction in the face of truth. Many people are unaware (or not knowing) the truth about God; this is considered to be ignorance. On the other hand, I did know and I was aware of the truth about God, and yet I still chose my own path; this is considered to be rebellion.

I was raised "Christian" and spent most of my childhood playing church and doing the religious thing without having a real relationship with God. I knew about Jesus, but knowing about someone and actually knowing them are very different things. In essence, I was in church, but the church wasn't in me. I would grow in size and stature, but not in spiritual maturity.

At nearly 7ft tall I was often asked, "do you play basketball?" I wasn't athletic, but I had a musical gift. I used the musical gift for ministry as a kid, yet as I neared adulthood and completed college, I endeavored to use the gift of music to become famous. I loved the gift more than the gift giver, and I wanted to exalt myself over the only one worthy of receiving glory. Of course, I didn't realize what I was doing at the time. I just wanted to be successful— and in this process I created music and a persona to be idolized; I desired to be larger than life for the world to appreciate, adore, and sadly enough, even worship. Humans were not designed to carry fame or glory, and I would have to find this out the hard way. I don't think God was pleased, yet I believe he allowed it. The music industry would unknowingly become my ministry training ground.

In 1995, This Is How We Do It was my very first song as a signed recording artist on Def Jam Records, and it was a number one hit. Today, over 25 years later, the song is deemed one the top 100 greatest party records of the last century! Throughout my career I would have several other number one records for myself and would even become a renown songwriter for other artists, garnering accolades, awards and achievements that would be considered extremely successful according to the world's standards. I can also honestly say on the other side of that journey, that success without significance is insubstantial. I am a living witness that you can have everything and still have nothing.

In other words, doing life without Jesus isn't really living; it's merely existing.

I would experience a life of great highs and many times even deeper lows. For every big song the world celebrated, behind the scenes and apart from the will of God I was consumed by alcohol and vices. My wife Kristin and I would experience the loss of a child, the burning of a home, and nearly the destruction of our marriage. There were so many ups and downs; and although I cherished the moments when we were on top of the world, I was too spiritually immature to recognize that our mountaintop moments were only a gift from God to see how to make it through the next valley.

If you are reading this, we possibly have more in common than you can imagine. Our lives have now intersected because God pursued us and interrupted our lives as we knew it. He then re-introduced us to the love He had for us before the foundation of the world, and for some crazy reason we were compelled by that love to say "yes." We are now connected because at some point, we recognized that we are sons and daughters of God, joint heirs with Christ, adopted into a family that produces a bond closer than any blood relative. I said "yes" to the family of God, and you did too. In essence, by reading pastor Tommy's book we are having a small family reunion.

I'm sharing my testimony with you for three reasons. First, because "Urban D." is a great friend and I support him and his family in every significant thing they do toward leading people to Jesus and equipping them to have a substantial walk with Christ after choosing to follow him. After all, my commitment to follow Jesus Christ was the best decision that I have ever made. I've tasted success and traveled the world multiple times, yet everything I have done and experienced pales in comparison to what I have found in Jesus.

Secondly, I want to encourage you that you are able to take your Next step because you have already taken the first one! And you can take it from someone who knows, it's not about the destination—but the journey.

Lastly, when I was living what I thought was my "best life" and leading people away from God, I did it with enthusiasm, conviction and reckless abandon. After surrendering my heart completely to Jesus and allowing the Holy Spirit to live inside of me, how could I possibly give God anything less than what I gave to the world? How could I give you anything less than God's best given to me? So, I share with enthusiasm, conviction and reckless abandon that your spiritual journey means far more than inheriting heaven in the next life. We get to enjoy a taste of heaven here on the earth, right now in this life, as we leave the past in the past and venture into what God has next for your life and the lives you will now impact and influence.

You can have everything in this world, yet without Jesus, you're bankrupt;
You can have nothing in this world, yet with Jesus, you're the wealthiest person alive.

No matter where you are in life, I'm so glad we get to take the **NEXT** steps of our spiritual journeys together.

Montell Jordan
Husband, Father, Friend, Artist and Author
Executive Pastor at Victory World Church, Norcross GA

If you're checking this book out it lets me know that you have either started a relationship with Christ or you are requesting more information about it. If you're starting that relationship with your creator let me spark it off by saying congratulations! If you're searching, I encourage you to also read on and be open to what God will say to you. God created you with a specific purpose. There are over six billion people on this planet and no one has the same fingerprint or DNA as you. Before we discover that purpose we have to understand the big picture and what God has done for us by sending his son Christ. I know you may have a million and one things running through your mind right now, so I wanted to give you something that can help you take your first few steps in your journey following Christ.

What you'll find in the pages of this small book is my story of how I came to know Christ and became a Christian (A Christ-follower). I'll also share some very key decisions I had to make that really helped me as I started my relationship with God. I had a lot of issues in my life when I first started this journey. God has helped me work through many of them. There's a section that talks about real issues like doubt, abuse, sexuality and more. I know we live in a culture of questions. Questions are good. I have lots of them all the time! I included a section that tries to answer some questions I had early on in my walk with Christ. The last section of the book includes the first 7 chapters of the book of John from the New Testament. This will get you started to read a chapter each day as it shares about Christ's life and several things he taught during his ministry here on earth. It is written in a very easy to read translation, so you can understand it and get the most out of God's word as you read it. We encourage you to download the YouVersion Bible app and you can finish reading the last 14 chapters there and connect with a devotional or Bible reading plan that will help you keep learning and growing.

The Bible says, *"Therefore, if anyone is in Christ, he is a new creation; the old has gone, the new has come!"* So, if you've made a sincere decision to follow Jesus Christ and have asked Him to forgive you of your sins and turn from your old ways, then according to God, you are a new creation! This is incredibly exciting news! If you're anything like I was... I needed to get rid of my old ways! I desperately needed a fresh start. Real life starts now. Anything before knowing Christ was just simply existing, but knowing God and walking with Him on the daily is REAL living! I look forward to seeing you on this journey and watching you discover what God has **NEXT**...

FROM RAPPER TO PASTOR... MY STORY

Tommy "Urban D." Kyllonen

The majority of my childhood and teenage years was spent growing up in the Philadelphia area. It's funny because my spiritual journey actually started even before I left my mother's stomach! My dad was pastor, so even the very night my mother went into contractions to have me she was in a church service. So as you can imagine I grew up in and around the church. But as I grew into my teenage years I soon realized there were these two worlds I lived in that didn't seem to blend very often. Growing up in an urban setting with hip-hop being the cultural identity of my generation... it soon became more real and attractive than what I was hearing at church. I believed in God and knew He was real, but the draw of the streets was becoming stronger and stronger. There was nobody I could relate to around my age that was living an authentic life for Christ. Again, I believed in God, but it seemed if I was going to be a Christian I couldn't be myself. That misconception pushed me away. It led to several years as a teen where I was made to attend church (parent's rules), but I wasn't truly living it out. I wanted to taste what the world had to offer and figured I could maybe give God a try when I got older. In the meantime I was playing sports, chasing money and picking up a mic to rap anytime I was given the chance.

Towards the end of my senior year of high school I began to get restless inside. There were actually several nights where I couldn't fall asleep until 3 or 4 in the morning as I was wrestling with what my future would hold. People were constantly asking me what college I was going to attend or what kind of career I was going to get into. I was clueless. Up to that point it had been about basketball, rapping, hanging out, making money and having a girlfriend or two. I was living for the moment, and I knew my future was coming, but I kept putting it off trying to enjoy the moment. God began drawing me to Him. I couldn't ignore it. Finally one restless night as I laid in bed around 2:30am, I said out loud, "Alright, I'll do whatever you want me to! So tell me what it is so I can go to sleep!" No, God didn't speak to me audibly, but I did feel him telling me to go to Bible College the next year after high school. I argued for about another hour until I finally agreed and then fell asleep. I thought I was making God happy by doing what I felt He was leading me to do, but I still wasn't truly "following" Him.

Bible College brought new freedoms as I was several hours away from home and I had my own car and my own dorm room. Instead of this experience drawing me closer to God, it actually caused me to drift a little farther. During my first semester I quickly made several new friends and hung out with several old friends that had little or no relationship with God. By the second semester all this running from God was coming to a climax. Here I was in Bible College cheating, shoplifting, lying, clubbing and living a double lifestyle. One Monday morning I sat in the required chapel service and God really rocked me. As most others stood passionately singing to their creator I sat reflecting on my wild weekend. God had me ask myself "What am I doing at Bible College?" "Why am I even here?" I wondered, as I had no major declared. I was planning to possibly transfer my second year to pursue communications and television work or just get a job in the city. I was confused and unsettled. I was disappointed in myself for living this double life. God challenged me that day to recommit my life to Him and he would show me what was **NEXT**. I did.

I asked him for forgiveness and asked Him to help me to truly change this time.

Within the next few days things really did begin to change. I got involved in an urban youth ministry and a homeless ministry connected with the college. It was in the subways of Center City Philadelphia where I began to discover a glimpse of what God had for my future. I became a youth leader in that youth ministry and God awakened this passion inside of me to help young people. At the same time I had this love for Hip-Hop and I was ready to put the mic down and let it go. But, God soon made it clear that he wanted to use my gifts, talents and even my rapping to share His message. I started to write songs about my transformation and my new love for God.

I continued in Bible college, but I transferred my second year down south to Southeastern University in Lakeland, Florida. I pursued my BA Degree in Pastoral Theology with a concentration in youth ministry. Those first six months after my re-commitment to God were full of ups and downs. I found there were moments I was still holding onto several things from the past. But as I took my **NEXT** steps God began to chip away those things from my life and my desires and my character started to become more like Christ. Every time I messed up and fell, I would pick myself up and with God's help press forward on the journey. I'm going to share some of those steps in the next few pages.

> *"My life was a disaster / Came home to the master / Running from my call to be a pastor / Told God that's it / I'll submit / I'll even cease to spit / That's right about then my pen got lit / found my gifts / perfect fit / 92' I'll never forget / He took me up to the penthouse and outta the pit / It was a total eclipse of the heart / Brand new start / No more clips of the dark / My life was a canvas / And the creator was making beautiful art / Here's the beautiful part / He left a beautiful mark / I found true peace at home / True peace is known / When you find that Jesus Christ is on the throne!"*
> **Urban D. "Home" feat. Bobby Tinsley from Un.orthodox**

When I finished Bible College I came to Tampa to start the youth ministry at this new church called Crossover. They never had a youth ministry before and there was just 1 teenage girl. We started Basketball leagues and we did Hip-Hop Concerts and God used my own talents and passions to reach hundreds and hundreds of teenagers. I didn't put the mic down and stop rapping. I actually picked it up more and recorded two independent albums and then got signed to a national record label. I've went on to record 9 albums and went from being the youth pastor to being the lead pastor. It's been a crazy journey that I would have never dreamt or imagined, but when you keep taking your **NEXT** steps, God will blow your mind!

Maybe you grew up around church like me, or maybe you didn't. Either way most Americans have some type of belief in God or a higher power. But, there is a big difference between faith and belief. There are many things we believe without putting our faith in them at all. How many people that smoke believe it's not good for them? Most of them. But, for most of them it doesn't change their habits. How many people believe that being overweight isn't healthy? Most people do. Believing something is true and having the courage to take a step and walk in that truth are two totally different things. That's where faith comes into the picture! We can all say we believe... but actions speak louder than what? Words! Faith requires action! Faith is acting on the beliefs that we have. That was the change in my life. Before I just had belief, but when I truly started following Christ it became faith. I put my faith in Christ and really became a Christian. This wasn't suddenly becoming religious. Honestly, I already had that. I regularly went to church and tried to do certain things to please God, but there was no real relationship and no real connection. Real recognizes Real! All those years I wasn't being real. Even though I knew about Him, I didn't really know Him. When I began to see Him for who He really is and truly began to follow Him - He changed my life. If you're reading this, God has either done this in your life, or you're searching.

If you haven't prayed and started a relationship with God and you'd like to, I have a prayer written below that is similar to the prayer I prayed that day in my college chapel service. These words are not some magic formula. Instead, they are words that I hope express your feelings towards God, what He's beginning to do already and what you would like Him to do in your life. If that's where you're at, I invite you to talk to God and pray:

"Dear heavenly father, thank you for drawing me to you. Thank you for going after me and getting my attention. I'm sorry that I've tried to live my life my own way. I realize I messed up and I need you. I ask that you would forgive me for all the mistakes and all the wrong I've done. I thank you for sending your son Christ to die for my mistakes. I believe I can be reconnected with you because of Christ's sacrifice and his resurrection. Help me to follow you and live out your plan for my life. Thank you for loving me and not giving up on me.
In Jesus name I pray, Amen."

If you sincerely prayed that prayer, then you have invited the God of the universe to begin working in your life. But, it's so much more than just one prayer. Following Christ is a lifestyle and a life long process. If you prayed that prayer and meant it then that is just the first step in your spiritual journey. I'm excited and honored to have been part of the process. I pray that the following pages will encourage and inspire you. I pray that they will serve you as a path that many of us have taken in our own journeys as we walk together with God and discover what's **NEXT**...

The beginning of your spiritual journey can definitely be a challenging and sometimes confusing season. You might be wondering what I did **NEXT** after I got serious with God. There were actually 5 **NEXT** steps that I took that helped me stay on track and really begin to grow in my faith. Some of these came naturally for me and others took some real discipline. I encourage you to implement these in your life. Of course these steps aren't some secret formula, but if you're sincere in your decision to follow Christ you should have a desire to begin to take these steps. If you're like me, as you take them you'll probably find that some will be automatic and some will take work, but as you apply these things they will take you to the **NEXT** level.

I TALKED WITH GOD EVERYDAY.

New Christ-followers regularly tell me that they don't know how to pray. It's a common feeling and a common misconception. If you're reading this it's safe for me to assume you know how to have a conversation with someone. That's exactly what prayer is... a conversation. It's a conversation with your creator. Sometimes we make prayer out to be something that is only for the super spiritual or those who have been a Christian for a long time. We may have heard prayers where they use a certain voice or use words like "thee" and "thou" and they repetitively say God's name a bunch of times. Jesus didn't pray like that! He didn't teach his disciples to pray like that either. In a discussion about prayer, Jesus said, *"And when you come before God, don't turn that into a theatrical production either. All these people making a regular show out of their prayers, hoping for stardom! Do you think God sits in a box seat? Here's what I want you to do: Find a quiet, secluded place so you won't be tempted to role-play before God. Just be there as simply and honestly as you can manage. The focus will shift from you to God, and you will begin to sense His grace."*
(Matthew 6:5-6 Message Bible)

So don't get all caught up in the words you use. God knows your heart. He wants to hear from you. I have two daughters and I remember when they were just learning to talk. As they learned to talk I wasn't concerned so much about what words they said, but what their heart was saying. I was so excited to hear them communicating with me! God is excited to hear from us. This is a relationship. If you have a relationship with someone, but you never take out time to talk with them and build with them then the relationship will soon die out or just remain at the surface level. So, take that step to spend some time with God and talk to him each day. You still might be wondering... what should I say? You can first start off with thanking him for some good things that have happened in your life. Even if we are going through a rough season, there are still some good things we can point to whether that is our family, our job, our food, our friends. Prayer should start out with gratitude. God also wants us to bring our needs to him and the needs of others. We can also bring our questions and express how we are feeling. Prayer really can change things. Many times God uses it to change us. Talking with God each day keeps you connected and growing in your journey with him.

I LEARNED ABOUT GOD EVERYDAY.

I've always been a visual learner, so I wasn't big into reading. Many people don't read a lot of books as there are so many ways to get information and most of us have shorter attention spans due to the way we now consume media. That's why we made this **"NEXT"** book small, easy to read and broken into sections so you can easily digest it. We also have it available in an audio book form online if that is easier for you. We can learn through so many forms of media, but what we are learning about is the important thing. As I grew in my relationship with God I've learned to become more of a reader and I now really enjoy it. We have to be intentional to take time out to learn about God and the biggest way we can do that is through the Bible. The Bible is God's love letter to us. It's full of amazing true stories of how God worked in the lives of people throughout history. It shows us how to live our lives and contrary to what many people think it is very relevant and full of things that we can apply to our everyday lives.

Just as you are taking the step to spend some time praying each day you should connect some time where you are learning more about His word. Maybe you can't always get into reading, but you learn better through audio. There are lots of great Audio Bibles you can listen to. One that I would highly recommend is available on a free App called *"Streetlights"*. It has urban artists reading the scripture in the NLT version. They took some of the top producers and put some great beats and soundscapes underneath of it. I had the honor of being part of the project and reading the book of Galatians. So download the app and listen to it in your car on your way to work or before you go to bed at night. You can also download the free "Youversion" app and have the Bible right at your fingertips anytime. There are several great devotionals and reading plans available on there. It has been downloaded by hundreds of millions of people. We included the first 7 chapters of the Gospel of John connected with this book as a great place to start as it shares the life and words of Christ. Make a habit to regularly learn about God through His word. I began to do this nearly every day and it helped me see new things and draw closer to God. There were many times I was struggling with something and what I read that day in the Bible spoke directly into what I was going through.

I WENT TO CHURCH EVERY WEEK.

This is a key step that a lot of people miss as they are new in their walk with God. Going to church every week isn't the thing that will change you as you heard my story of growing up around church and still not being real with it. But, as you make a true commitment to God it's vital to grow with others. God wired us that we need to be in community and we need to worship and serve together. When I got real with God, suddenly my experience at church became something I looked forward to as I sang songs from my heart to God, I opened up the Bible and I heard teaching that helped me take my **NEXT** steps. I built relationships with people and I had a place to use my talents that God had given me to help others also connect with Him. I quickly noticed if I missed a Sunday or two I became more distant from God and felt disconnected from the community of people I was building with. It was easier to slip back into my old habits. I realized I was missing that special time in God's presence with my church family and being able to grow in the teaching and fellowship with them.

God created the church. It was his idea. Jesus calls the church his bride. Who is the church? People that have a relationship with Christ. So… it's not just a place, it's a group of people that together are on a mission. They meet regularly… but what kind of space they meet in is not important. The church I lead meets in an old Toys R' Us store. I've been to churches that meet at schools, hotels, movie theaters, houses or traditional cathedrals. Where you meet is not important, but the fact that you meet and what you do when you meet is important. *Acts 2:42-27* talks about the purposes of what the church is supposed to be about. I love the church. I am passionate about the church. Sometimes it's awesome. Sometimes it's messy. If you are looking for a perfect church you will never find it… because it's full of people and none of us are perfect.

Our world seems to be getting busier all the time. There is information coming at us from a million different directions and our schedules are more packed than ever, but we must take time out to intentionally develop our relationship with God. When we carve out time to attend church it helps us get grounded as we worship God, hear his word preached and we build with other Christians. If we don't do this… no one will do it for us! We have to protect our time and prioritize it.

I BUILT SOME NEW FRIENDSHIPS.

I always had lots of friends. Some of them were real Christians, some claimed to be Christians and some were definitely not. I had spent most of my time with those that just claimed to be Christians and those that I knew weren't following God at all. That was the group I was attracted to as we were into the same things. As I truly started following God I knew I needed to strengthen some of those relationships with some of the real Christ followers in my life. I also began to seek out some new friends from my church. These were people that were really going hard after God. I wanted to learn from them and see what their passion was all about. As I got involved in serving in ministry I soon had several new people to help me in my journey. Some of them were older and although I thought I didn't relate to them, I felt attracted to their love for God. Soon I found there were actually many things we had in common. They were there to help me with my problems, give me solid advice and to pray for me. All these people soon became a very important support system as I knew they loved God and they loved me as well.

I didn't turn my back on my old friends, but I began to spend a lot less time with them as there were many things they did and said that I was trying to get away from. There were times I tried to convince myself that I was strong enough to be around them more then I should have, but I found myself being negatively influenced by them instead of helping them. As my relationship with God grew stronger I reconnected more with some of my old friends as I was in a better place to encourage, challenge, influence and help them. Who you hang out with is always vital in shaping who you are and who you'll be. My mom used to always warn me on this point and I always argued, but I have to give it up to her... she was right. The old saying goes something like - *"Show me your friends and I'll show you your future".* Who are your friends?

I STARTING SERVING AND GIVING BACK

We're all selfish by nature. Sure, we may have moments when we help someone or give to something, but many times we do that because it makes us feel good. As our relationship with God grows and we realize what He's given us, our heart begins to change. When we hang around others that are serving and giving it begins to influence us in a positive way. Our very nature gets transformed. The Bible says that *"if anyone is in Christ, he is a new creation; the old has gone, the new has come!" (2 Corinthians 5:17)* As He changed my heart I felt compelled to give back and serve and help others as people had helped me. As I spent time learning about God each day and reading His word I found that Christ even considered himself a servant. He promoted that we serve one another. That's counter-cultural! The media promotes that when we make it we should have people serving us. Hip-Hop artists, professional athletes and celebs live a lifestyle on the screen that is full of personal assistants, body guards and an entourage of people serving their every need right down to the blue M&M's in their backstage dressing room.

As my eyes were open to reality, I began to see that serving others was what it's really all about. I started with some things that were simple like helping clean up or set up chairs or give some people a ride home from church. Some things were specific to my talents as I got involved playing drums and helping out in the youth group with teens. As my relationship with God continued to grow I started leading some things and pouring into others. Today I have the privilege and honor to serve and lead Crossover Church. Giving back and serving is so rewarding at every level! From setting up some chairs to now being the lead pastor and speaking into people's lives and sometimes still setting up chairs - it's all good! If you don't learn to get involved and give back you'll soon find you get stuck in your growth! Sometimes I have people tell me they feel like they're not growing, and usually a big connection to that is they're not serving and they're not giving back. Something supernatural begins to happen when we begin to put Christ's words into action and we start loving our neighbor as ourselves. We get activated. At Crossover Church the people that serve are called "Activators".

I encourage you to start serving and giving back and you'll watch God do things in you and use you like you've never imagined!

_____

_____

_____

_____

_____

_____

_____

_____

_____

_____

_____

_____

_____

_____

_____

_____

Most of us have issues but many times we don't want to admit it. We don't want to reveal our weakness. We're worried about what other people will think. We can feel alone, but there are several people right here at this church that have gone through the same things. God knows about our issues. He knows our about our past. This doesn't scare Him. This doesn't scare us. Many of us have some rough backgrounds. Don't let your background or your current issues hold you back from taking your **NEXT** steps in your walk with God. I talk to so many people that always feel like they can't come to God because of certain issues they have in their life. Our creator wants us to come to Him just as we are - with all our issues, drama and baggage. We can't fix those things. We'll never get cleaned up enough to make ourselves ready to get with Him. He wants us to come to Him and be open and willing and He'll help us make the changes and deal with our issues.

I'VE GOT DOUBT ISSUES

If we're honest we've all had some doubt about God at some times in our lives. Even Christ's very own disciples had doubt issues of who He really was throughout their time with Him even though they saw the miracles right in front of them! After Jesus Christ was crucified His disciple Thomas doubted that He had been raised from the dead. Thomas had some legit reasons to doubt the claims of the other disciples. Sometimes life gets pretty crazy and we have some pretty legit reasons to question, wonder and doubt. Sometimes awful circumstances or painful suffering cause us to ask that huge question:

"If God is really good, why does he let _____ (fill in the blank) happen?"

There are times we don't feel God's presence. It may just be logical questions that creep up and shake our faith. Like Thomas, we've got our own doubts. But do we deal with our doubts like Thomas did? Or do we hide away our questions and refuse to talk about them to others? It just gives them power over us. It lets doubt take over... it makes us feel alone. It can turn us into fakes.

Thomas was real with his crew about his doubts. He didn't front like he believed. He was authentic and raw. And when the time was right, Jesus met Thomas right where he was. Jesus showed up on the scene and invited Thomas to literally stick his finger right in the nail-holes in Jesus' hands. Jesus didn't get in his face and call him out. No, instead Jesus provided the proof that he needed to believe. And that proof completely changed the course of Thomas' life, as he knelt before Jesus and cried out, *"You are my Lord and my God!" (John 20:28)*.

God isn't afraid of our doubts. He can handle it. In fact, He welcomes when you express your real and honest questions. Look throughout the scriptures and you'll find people crying out to Him with their questions and doubts. God wants the authentic you - even if that means telling Him you feel like a fake or you wonder if He's real or you question things happening in the world.

Just like he did for Thomas, when the time is right, God will provide the proof you need, or will give you a sense of peace about your questions, or will give you the guts and desire to make your faith even more real. So, you've got a choice to make: turn to God and to your Christian friends with transparency about your spiritual questions and struggles... or let doubt strangle and weaken your faith.

In this short space it's hard to address the deep pain felt by people who have been abused or victimized by others. The percentage of people who have suffered abuse is always much higher in the city. So many have unresolved issues of brokenness, hurt, shame and confusion. You may have been abused by a friend or family member that you trusted. You may have told someone and they didn't believe you or didn't take any action. You may even be feeling like it was partially your fault. This may have led to you thinking you'll never recover or break free from these emotions. I want to encourage you that freedom is possible. Healing is possible.

You know who understands what you're feeling? Jesus Christ. He suffered big time and He didn't deserve it. They spit on Him, called Him out and lied about Him. He was beat down and went through horrific torture. Cruel, ignorant people did this to Him. He didn't deserve any of it. So, whatever has been done to you and whatever secret pain you carry because of what someone else did to you - you can turn to Jesus because He understands better than anyone else what it is to suffer! Jesus can help you carry the heavy burden of brokenness that you feel inside. It may seem hard to believe, but He can bring healing to that brokenness!

Yes, there is a lot of evil in our world and sometimes that evil takes the form of horrible acts committed against others. If you've been a victim of some evil act - it's not your fault! And be encouraged... because your story is not finished. That abuse and that evil wants to stick around and keep hurting you. If you let it... it will define who you are... it will define your future. But Christ wants to rescue you from that hurt and set you free! He has a totally different story line for you.

Turn towards Jesus Christ.

See His suffering.

See His blood.

See His tears.

See His heartache.

Listen to His words to us:
"If you are tired from carrying heavy burdens, come to me and I will give you rest."(Matthew 11:28)

I'VE GOT SEXUAL ISSUES

Verse One:
Peep the culture's mentality / Saturated by sexuality / Attracted by sensuality / Fantasizing a false reality / Here's the technicality / We're trying to fill a spot created for spirituality / It's grown to epic proportions / It's turned a beautiful thing into an ugly contortion / Take caution / When you browsing on the web late nights / Cuz there's over 300 million porn sites / It starts with small bites / But beware your appetite can grow / Statistics will show / It's an epidemic that over 50 million Americans now know / Cuz their addicted/ They can't evict it / It's wrecked their expectations – their afflicted / It's big business / Bigger than all pro sports put together / $12 Billion dollars (watch out) – temptation is clever /

Verse Two:
Sex sells and the culture buys / From music, to cars, to French Fries / Legs, breasts, and thighs / Marinating in your thoughts – it ain't wise / From Tims and Jeans – To suits and ties / It all starts with the eyes / For the girls and especially for the guys / Lust entices with the tantil - eyes / It's no surprise / We try to take something that ain't ours - we plagiar - eyes / In our mind we try to re-shape reality – we love to custom – eyes / But the result we despise / The consequences come in and wreck us with the vandal – eyes / Don't fall for the lies / Don't fall for the disguise / Let's stand up together and rize / and open our spiritual eyes / See the truth – see the proof – let's unite and mobile – eyes /
from Urban D.'s song "Temptation" from The Un.orthodox album.

Everyday we're bombarded with countless sexual images. It seems to be a major thread in the fabric of nearly everything we look at; commercials, billboards, magazines, TV shows, Youtube clips, music videos, etc. The culture is constantly influencing us on this subject. In essence they are educating us! But, the majority of what they're teaching us is a false version of how it really is.

Have you ever wanted to buy something really nice, but you couldn't afford it? All the time, right? You know the latest style or the hottest brand name that's out there grabbing everyone's attention? Many of us have found a way we can still get it... not by stealing it, but by getting the imitation aka the bootleg version. Nowadays they do a great job with making the bootleg look exactly like the real thing! Sometimes the bootleg version can even look better as it comes out in unique colors or styles that the real version never even came out in. A few years ago I was walking around at the local flea market and I saw some Jordan's that caught my eye. I've always loved Jordans and have owned several pairs over the years. For all my sneaker heads you'll feel me on this. I've always wanted to get a pair of the 4's and I saw this pair with a brown and tan color way. I'm personally into the earth tone colors, so I was like - Yo! I picked them up and they were suede! They looked official. I asked the dude how much, and to my surprise they were only $60! What? He asked me my size, so I told him and he brought out an official Jordan box with tags and papers. I tried them on and ended up taking them home! Over the next year or so I had lots of compliments on those shoes with people constantly telling me how dope they were and asking where I got that color and how much they cost. But, soon something strange started to happen. The outside of the shoe still looked great, but the inside sole started falling apart, to the point where there was a hole going all the way to the rubber. I knew something was up, but I got some gel insoles to put inside to solve the problem and it was all good. But, a few months later I noticed that the entire bottom of the right shoe had a crack all the way across and it was exposing the inside of the shoe. If I stepped in a puddle the whole inside of the shoe would instantly get wet. Then I knew for sure - they were bootleg! I fell for the bootleg - lol!

The version of Sex that the culture is selling us is almost always a bootleg version. It looks good on the outside, but the inside will quickly fall apart! It sometimes even looks better and comes out in different styles and flavors than we've ever seen before (it's called porn). It's easier and it's cheaper! But, in the end it will always let you down. Sex is a beautiful thing that God created and he wants us to enjoy it, but in the right context aka the way He planned it. In the very first book of the Bible it says, "For this reason a man will leave his father and mother and be united to his wife, and they will become one flesh." (Gen. 2:24) His plan for sex is between a man and a women in marriage. But, the culture will constantly push and promote a very different version to us. They make it look cool to sleep around with different people, view porn or experiment with someone of your own gender. What they don't tell you is that eventually it will leave you empty and emotionally wrecked. God doesn't set these standards in place because he doesn't want us to have fun. He does this because he cares about us and he knows how our emotions are wired because he made us. God knows that when we have sex with someone we leave a piece of our soul with that person. So many people have left so many pieces of themselves with others they are confused of who they are or what they really want.

The culture teaches us that pornography is normal, innocent and it doesn't hurt anyone. Porn is now as easily accessible as our cell phones. It can seem like no big deal at first, but porn quickly becomes very addictive and it changes the way that we think about our sexuality. It sets false expectations and makes us become very self-centered. Everyday it destroys relationships and ends marriages and leaves people empty, guilty and unhappy. Our culture will also promote that homosexuality is cool. Reality TV shows, movies and music videos have done a great job of making this lifestyle look normal, acceptable and even fun. But, it's a bootleg version and according to our creator it's not cool. It's not how how He intended it to be. In the Bible in both the Old Testament and New Testament it talks about how homosexuality is not natural, it's not normal, it's wrong.

You might be reading this now and feeling bad as you've fallen for the bootleg and messed up sexually in some areas. You may currently be struggling with lust, porn or homosexuality. First off, I want to remind you that God loves you so much! He cares greatly for you and has an incredible plan for your life. It's no accident you're reading this section on sexual issues... yes, the word SEX probably got your attention, but God drew you here to talk to you. Many times Christians and the church can be very quiet on this topic, but the scriptures have a lot to say about it. God created Sex to be a beautiful thing that a man and a woman enjoy in marriage, but culture took it and perverted it into something dirty that can cause us a lot of pain. If you are dealing with that pain, God can bring true healing and true change to your life. You have to admit where you're at, ask Him for help and then be willing to submit to Him and follow His standards. If this section is speaking to you and you know you need to change, I invite you right now to pause and pray this prayer:

"Dear God, I thank you for putting this book in front of me and speaking to me about a very real subject. I admit this is an area where I've struggled and made some mistakes. I believe you sent your son Christ to bring forgiveness for my mistakes. Today I ask for that forgiveness. I'm sorry. I know you love me and that you don't want me to stay the same, so please bring true change in my life. Bring healing in this area of my heart. Give me strength and discipline to follow your plans and to be careful about the things I look at and the things I listen to. Help me not to fall for the bootleg version, but to have eyes to see the truth. Help me to change my habits and honor you in everything I do. In Jesus name - Amen."

We are emotional beings. That's how our creator wired us. But, there are times when some of us live totally by our emotions and we let them control us. We all get discouraged sometimes. We all have moments when we feel down. It's normal. It's part of being a broken, sin-affected human being. We live in a sin-sick world where there are plenty of depressing things out there - just turn on the news. But, if you find yourself wrestling with the question of what you're worth... if you're overcome by discouragement, if you've started cutting or stopped eating or have thoughts about ending your life - find someone to talk to! Satan is a deceiver and nothing makes him happier than getting us to buy into the lie that we're worthless and that life is hopeless. It's his way of trying to cancel out the message of Christ. It's his way of trying to mute God's words about how much He loves us. 1 Corinthians 6:20 says, "God paid a great price for you." He didn't pay it because He had to. He didn't pay it because He didn't know what you were really like. God paid the ultimate price because you are precious to Him. God knows the real you with all your issues. And it was for that real you that Jesus suffered and died on the cross. To Him, you're worth every second of the pain He went through.

So, You may come from a family with a history of depression issues. You may come from generations of mistakes and drama. You may have grown up in a neighborhood where hopelessness was the norm. All of this on top of the daily weight of life may make you feel like you'll always be stuck. You may be in the middle of a crisis right now. Every crisis gives you the opportunity to change. You are now following the God who created everything. With Him, your opportunities are limitless. You can now fight these depression issues and beat them with God's help. I've seen several people that were clinically depressed on all kinds of medication who found Christ and were soon cured. Talk to God and share your heart and give Him your problems and watch how much lighter it will make you feel. I've had some very dark depressing times in my life where I paused and spent time with God and then walked away suddenly feeling so much better. The reality was nothing physically changed at that moment, but I was able to see the big picture and trust Him and believe that the change would come and He would take care of me... and He always has! If you're struggling in this area I encourage you to talk to someone who loves you and share your issues with them. Tell that person how you've been feeling and ask them to pray for you and check up on you. Whenever you start to hear the lies that discourage you or make you feel worthless, remind yourself of God's message of love to you.

I'VE GOT FINANCIAL ISSUES

Close to 80% of Americans live paycheck to paycheck. We live in the richest country on the planet, but yet our country has the most debt (the people and the government). We also have the highest rate of depression and people on anti-depressants. Isn't that crazy? We are the richest, but yet we are the most in debt and the most depressed in the world. So if you have financial issues, you are actually in the majority. But, God doesn't want us to stay there. He has a blueprint for us to have financial freedom. It doesn't mean we're all going to be millionaires. Some Christians can teach what is called the "Prosperity Gospel." Some teach that everyone is going to be rich and if you just give to their ministry it will all fall into place. Unfortunately, this is false teaching and it gives churches and pastors a bad reputation. The truth is that God does want all of us to prosper, but it's going to look different for each of us. Some are called to be teachers, some are called to be construction workers, some are called to be CEO's of a company. It doesn't matter how much money we make, it's that we are in the center of God's plan for our lives and that we are being good managers of what he has given us. When we truly put God first in our lives, he will always provide everything we need.

Jesus talked a lot about money and possessions because he knew it was a big deal to people. It can be a blessing or a burden. I encourage you to read Matthew chapter 6 as there are several powerful things that Jesus shared. In verse 24 he told us that we can't serve both God and money. If you are constantly chasing after money, it will be difficult to truly follow God. Jesus also made it clear that when we store up treasures here on earth they will rust, rot and can be stolen. He encouraged us to store up treasures in heaven where that can't happen. How do we store up treasure in heaven? We serve and we give of our time, talent and resources. Those are things we can pay forward into eternity. Jesus also said in Matthew 6:21, "Wherever your treasure is, there the desires of your heart will also be." If you ever bought a new car, you are cleaning it, taking care of it. You don't let anyone eat in it. You are thinking about it. Why? Because you put a lot of your treasure in it. You worked hard to pay for it. In the same way when you put your time, talent and treasure into God's work and into the local church - the desires of your heart will follow. You will take ownership in things that will last forever.

"I'll be honest, it was hard at first / Even though we say we want to put God first / Because we all struggle with this material thirst / But, you can't take nothing when you get in the hearse / We only get to hold it for a minute / real easy to spend it / But real hard to give it / It's real hard to live / But, God can take your little and bridge it / Multiply it double digit / I'm a witness / I've learned generosity / It becomes intuitive in God's economy / now - it's all up in my - I get so excited to give back and love my city /
Urban D. - "Give, Multiply, Grow, Repeat" (Love Our City album)

We did a series about Finances at Crossover Church in February and March of 2019 called "God Over Money". I encourage you to go and check it out on our church youtube channel - ***www.youtube.com/crossover813***

Maybe you've made some mistakes in the past that led you to get locked up or lose your license or go on probation. God loves us and forgives us, but there are still consequences to many of the mistakes we've made and we have to deal with them correctly. There are usually two extremes to legal issues. The first is where some people are so hard on themselves they feel like God can never use them. They are ashamed of their past and they try to hide it and never say anything to anyone. Jesus loves to use people that messed up. Look at some of His disciples. A lot of them had some serious issues, but He gave them a chance. Look at the person that wrote the majority of the New Testament. His name used to be Saul and he was known for throwing Christians in jail, torturing them and even killing some of them. One day he was on a mission to a city called Damascus to find some Christians there and take them out. Jesus stopped him dead in his tracks, blinded him and gave him instructions on what was **NEXT**. Saul's name was changed to Paul and he soon became one of the biggest Christian leaders in history. That's crazy isn't it? God used a murderer to change the world! So, if you're still beating yourself up about what you did and how you're not worthy for God to work in your life... look at Paul!

The second extreme is that some people continue to have a chip on their shoulder and try to take the short cuts and do things they shouldn't. They don't show up for court dates, probation appointments, they drive without a license or skip out on their child support payments. They do these things and sometimes actually have the nerve to pray and ask God to help them not get caught. When we start this journey with God He wants our character to become like His. When we break the law or try to bend the rules that's not like His character. He wants us to be responsible and to have integrity. I've many times watched God do miracles when it came to people's legal issues, but it usually was with people that were making the right choices and choosing to follow through and honor their commitments which showed they were honoring God.

We're not here to judge you as there are many people at our church that have had lots of legal issues. We're here to help you and cheer for you to take your **NEXT** steps. There are many times I've been downtown at the courthouse testifying for someone from our church and even more often writing letters about how their character has changed. We want to encourage you to honor God and follow through with what's required. There are several miracle stories at Crossover of people that went from hustling in streets to now working at a solid job, learning a trade and some even running their own businesses. Take it a day at a time, be patient and take your **NEXT** step.

_____

_____

_____

_____

_____

_____

_____

_____

_____

_____

_____

_____

_____

_____

_____

1. WHO IS GOD? WHERE DID HE COME FROM?

God is the creator of the universe. So when you think about the massive size of the universe you can understand how it's difficult to fully describe the creator of everything. God came down to earth in the person of Jesus. Jesus said, "To see me is to see the father." (John 14:9 Message). John was one of Jesus' disciples and he said, "God is love." (1 John 4:8). God's very nature is love. Although God is very complex the Bible does break down many of His characteristics. It shares that God is all-knowing (Psalms 147:4-5), ever present (Jeremiah 23:23-24), and all-powerful (Isaiah 40:25-26). The creator of everything actually wants to have a relationship with you and me. We're the pinnacle of His creation. That's why God asks us to call Him father.

The second part of the question is a tough one... where did He come from? My daughter first asked this when she was around 7 years old. What did I say? He always was here. That's hard for us to wrap our minds around as we look at everything having a beginning and an end. That's all we know as humans in a world where everything is born and dies. But, God exists outside of time and space. That's deep! That's a mystery. I'm excited that one day in heaven I'll be able to sit down with my creator and have Him fully break this down for me!

2. WHO IS JESUS?

God has revealed Himself in three persons: God the father, God the son and God the Holy Spirit. We believe in one God that has revealed Himself in these three distinct ways. This is also referred to as the Trinity. Jesus is God's son who came down and put on human flesh. The Bible says, "For the law was given through Moses, but God's unfolding love and faithfulness came through Jesus Christ. No one has ever seen God. But the unique one, who is himself God, is near to the father's heart. He has revealed God to us." (John 1:18 NLT) Jesus came to die for our sins and create a way for us to get reconnected back to God the father. Throughout His life He also showed us God's character and His nature. "Christ is the visible image of the invisible God. He existed before anything was created and is supreme over all creation, for through Him God created everything in the heavenly realms and on earth. He made the things we can see and the things we can't see - such as thrones, kingdoms, rulers and authorities in the unseen world. Everything was created through Him and for Him. He existed before anything else, and He holds all creation together." (Colossians 1:15-17 NLT)

3. WHO IS THE HOLY SPIRIT?

When you become a Christ-follower God's spirit is now with you. He lives in every Christian and is there to guide you and direct you in your everyday life and give you discernment as you make decisions. The Holy Spirit is constantly at work in our lives as Christians to draw us closer to God. There are times you'll feel convicted about doing something wrong... that is God's spirit at work in you to help you make better choices. When He's working in our lives real change begins to happen.

Paul wrote, *"But the Holy Spirit produces this kind of fruit in our lives: love, joy, peace, patience, kindness, goodness, faithfulness, gentleness, and self-control. There is no law against these things!" (Galatians 5:22-23 NLT)*

The spirit is also there to empower us to be a witness and represent Him wherever we go: on our block, our city, our country and even over seas. Acts 1:8 talks about this empowerment as it says, "You will receive power when the Holy Spirit comes on you; and you will be my witnesses in Jerusalem and in all Judea and Samaria, and to the ends of the earth." In Acts the Holy Spirit empowered this uneducated group of Galilean Christians to take the message of Christ from their local neighborhood to their region and eventually all over the world! So no matter where you are from or what your issues are - if you have a relationship with Christ, you now have the Holy Spirit working in your life to lead you and empower you to accomplish everything God has **NEXT** for you.

4. WHO IS SATAN?

Our culture has a lot of misconceptions of who Satan is, what he does and what he looks like. The typical thought is the guy rockin' the red suit complete with the horns and pitchfork. But, if we look in the scriptures we find a very different picture of Satan. Back in the day he was actually an angel who served God as the music director. His name was "Lucifer". He was gifted, talented and beautiful. Others noticed this and soon he grew more and more prideful and started seeking the spotlight. He wanted to be worshipped like God. God challenged him and he rebelled and was kicked out of heaven (Check out Isaiah 14) and became known as Satan. A third of the angels followed Satan and were also thrown out of heaven.

Satan is a created being with limited power. His greatest weapon is the lie. He can make us seem like he is way bigger and way more powerful than he actually is! God's spirit is greater than any of his scams. Satan is all about trying to tempt believers into not following God's plan for our lives. He's been about this since the very beginning of creation (Genesis 3). John 10:10 calls Satan a thief that "comes only to steal and kill and destroy." Jesus says, "I have come that they may have life and have it to the full!" Most of us have been robbed before. Somebody has probably stolen something from us at some point in our lives. We know it's a terrible feeling that brings frustration and anger. Recognize that Satan is trying to rob you of something way more important than your stuff.

5. HAS THE BIBLE BEEN CHANGED?

This is a question that has especially plagued the urban community. For years there has bee false rumors about this that have been spread from skeptics and those of other religions. Today with th unlimited amount of information on the internet there has been numerous youtube clips, blogs and websites that have created all kinds of stories, theories and lies. We believe the Bible is God's word and is 100% accurate. How can we be sure of that? Here's some facts that logically lead us to that conclusic The Bible was written by over 40 authors on 3 continents in 3 languages. They came from all different walks of life: Kings, Military leaders, Peasants, Philosophers, Fisherman, Tax Collectors, Poets, Musician Scholars and Shepherds. With this incredibly diverse background it still flows with incredible Harmony. It's been the best selling book ever as it has sold billions of copies. The Bible has been translated into 2,200 languages which is over 90% of the literate world.

But how do we know it's accurate? We have to look at several things. How many copies of the original manuscripts do we have (so we can compare and make sure nothing has been changed)? In ancient literature Homer's "The Illiad" comes in second place with the most manuscripts in existence today with 643 copies. The New Testament comes in first place with over 24,000 copies. These manuscripts have incredible accuracy as scholars have compared all the copies and have seen that they do line up in their translations. There were people that dedicated their lives to making sure these manuscripts were protected and re-copied again and again with precision accuracy.

There is also an overwhelming amount of evidence of early historical writers (some were Christians and some were not) that verify many things written in scripture. Archaeology has also becon a huge form of evidence the past few hundred years. Nelson Glueck is a famous Jewish Archeologist that said, "It may be stated categorically that no archeological discovery has ever contradicted a biblica reference. In addition William Albright is known as one of the world's greatest archaeologists and he states, "Discovery after discovery has established the accuracy of innumerable details and has brought increased recognition to the Bible as a source of history."

Another proof of the Bible's accuracy and inspiration is that it tells the future of persons, places and things that had not yet occurred at the time it was written. There are several prophecies in the Old Testament that then take place in the New Testament as it described all the details. You can definitely find unreliable sources that you can't confirm, (like youtube, blogs, websites, etc.) that will tell you differently, but if you look at documented, reliable writings with solid facts - you'll soon find th Bible is 100% accurate. There was an agnostic/atheist named Lee Strobel who was on a quest to prove the Bible wasn't true. He traveled the world. A few years into his research he came to the conclusion the Bible was real and he became a Christ-follower! Now he travels the world spreading the truth. I recommend his book which is now also been made into a movie "The Case For Christ". Josh McDowell also has a great book to check out "The New Evidence that demands a verdict." We had a series at Crossover Church called "Fake News" and one of the weeks was confronting the fake news that the Bible had been changed. You can search this on our youtube channel (***www.youtube.com/crossover813***).

6. WHAT TRANSLATION OF THE BIBLE SHOULD I READ?

If you go to your local book store you'll quickly see there are many different translations of the Bible. This can be confusing as you may wonder which one should you should pick. In this short explanation I can't possibly give the details on each of the most popular translations. The bottom line is that these versions are saying the same thing. It's not like you have have one version saying Jesus rose from the dead and another saying He didn't. Translations vary for a number of different reasons: some translations (Like the New American Standard, The King James and The New King James versions) are written in a word for word format. They tell us exactly what was written in the Hebrew Old Testament and Greek New Testament. Other translations (Like the New International Version, New Living Translation, and the Contemporary English Version) use what is called "Dynamic Equivalent" when they translate from the original languages. They not only translate the words, but they also provide the meaning of the words as they were used in their original form. This can help some readers better understand the original meaning. There are also paraphrase versions (like The Message) where the thought behind the original languages is written in today's language to become more readable for people. Either way, the end result is the same - they are seeking to communicate God's heart through the pages of scripture.

The choice of what translation to read from is yours. I personally own several translations and read from several different ones on a regular basis. When teaching at Crossover or other venues I generally use the NLT, NIV, ESV or sometimes The Message paraphrase as they are all easy to understand as I speak to a very diverse audience. I also personally enjoy using a Study Bible. They have notes on the bottom half of the page that breaks down the details from each verse. I have several Study Bibles in different translations. This can be a great help as you read and study the Bible and come across verses that you may not understand. I'm a history dude, so I also enjoy the detailed introductions that Study Bibles include at the beginning of each of the different books of the Bible. This helps to greater paint the picture of what was happening in culture at the time and who it was being written to and how we can properly apply it today. So, I encourage you to find a translation that you can understand and that you'll be comfortable to regularly read.

7. WHAT IS BAPTISM?

There is a big different between what is traditional and what is biblical. Our church may not be very traditional, but we strive to be biblical and do the things they did in the New Testament Church. Baptism is one of those biblical things that we celebrate at our church! It is the outward display of telling others you are now following Christ. Here's where a big misconception comes in... people think they have to have their act together to be baptized. No, if you have made a commitment to follow Christ and you believe the gospel - you're ready! There is no need to delay. When we look in the book of Acts people that believed were baptized that day! It is the outward symbol of your inward commitment. Every follower of Christ is actually commanded to be baptized. It's a symbolic act of our desire to follow Jesus by identifying with Him in His death, burial and resurrection through water baptism. *"Then Jesus came to them and said, 'All authority in heaven and on earth has been given to me. Therefore go and make disciples of all nations, baptizing them in the name of the Father and of the Son and of the Holy Spirit, and teaching them everything I have commanded you. And surely I am with you always, to the very end of the age.'" Matthew 28:18-20 (NIV)*

Don't get it twisted... getting baptized doesn't make you a Christian, but true Christians will get baptized. Some churches will baptize or sprinkle infants. At our church we look at the biblical model of Children getting dedicated with a special prayer (1 Samuel 2). We regularly do baby dedications in our services. When children or teenagers are old enough to understand the gospel and they make a decision to follow Christ, they then can be baptized in water. We encourage you to make this **NEXT** step if you haven't been baptized before or you're making a recommitment to God and you'd like to be baptized in front of your new church family. We regularly have baptism celebrations at our church services and baptize hundreds of new believers each year!

8. WHAT IS COMMUNION?

This is another biblical act that we do on a regular basis at our church. Communion (aka The Lord's Supper) began on the night before Jesus died on the cross. There was a Jewish feast happening called Passover. This feast celebrates God's deliverance of the Jewish people being released from slavery in Egypt. Every year Jews still observe this. Jesus and his closest friends were together that night eating and celebrating Passover. Jesus picked up some bread and broke it and compared it to His body, which would be broken for us. Then He picked up a glass of wine and compared it to His blood, which would be shed for us. The Bible breaks down the scene in Luke 22:19-20 and says, *"And He took bread, gave thanks and broke it, and gave it to them, saying, 'This is my body given for you; do this in remembrance of me.' In the same way, after the supper He took the cup, saying, 'This cup is the new covenant in my blood, which is poured out for you.'"*

As Christians we participate in communion to draw close to God and celebrate our faith. It is a time of personal spiritual inspection and a time of reflection and thanksgiving. It serves to remind us of the incredible price that God paid for us to have a relationship with Him. He paid with the life of His Son.

9. WHY IS THERE DEATH, SUFFERING AND VIOLENCE IN THE WORLD?

Various answers have been given over the course of history, but many answers can raise further questions. Have you ever noticed that everything on this planet is dying? Slowly, but surely it's dying. Everything has a beginning and an end. This isn't how it was at the beginning of creation. God put Adam in Charge (Genesis 1:28). When Adam disobeyed God he set in motion an entire series of events and changed the very nature of man and creation. Both were affected by sin. Creation was no longer a paradise, but became a place of thorns and thistles. In Genesis 3:17-19 God spoke to Adam because He and Eve ate from the tree; He told them, *"'Cursed is the ground because of you; through painful toil you will eat of it all the days of your life. It will produce thorns and thistles for you, and you will eat the plants of the field. By the sweat of your brow you will eat your food until you return to the ground, since from it you were taken; for dust you are and to dust you will return.'"* People became sinful and became haters of God. They became selfish and many became violent.

But, God has not left us alone in this fallen world. He sent His son to die on the cross so we can be reconnected back to Him. Christ's sacrifice provides that forgiveness from our sins and gives us eternal life. God redeems fallen people to accomplish His will. Suffering is the result of human sin. The world is not the way that God originally created it and because of that, all are vulnerable to the effects of sin in the world. Why do some suffer and others don't? Why do some have food and others don't? These are difficult questions to answer as we can't possibly see the big picture our creator does. We must keep in mind that our pain and suffering here on this planet is just temporary. It's like one tiny grain of sand on a beach in comparison with the rest of our time after this life. Revelation 21:4 says, *"He will wipe every tear from their eyes. There will be no more death or mourning or crying or pain, for the old order of things has passed away."*

10. HOW DO I KNOW I'M A CHRISTIAN?

The majority of people in America still would say they are a Christian. A Christian can be defined as someone who is following Christ. This can be quite confusing as many people that categorize themselves as Christians don't live at all like they are following Christ. We need to understand that we aren't automatically Christians because our parents or grandparents were or we went to church when we were younger or because we live in America. Becoming a Christian is a personal thing between you and your creator. A person becomes a Christian when their eyes are opened to the gospel and they ask Christ to forgive them for their sins. Our sins separate us from God. We're disconnected. It's not something we can fix. But, because of what Christ did by dying on the cross we can now be reconnected. When you believe this (the gospel) and ask for forgiveness and commit to follow Christ (and turn from your old ways) the Bible says you are now a Christian. The goal now is to follow Christ and live by His example. What is His example? This is why reading the Bible is so important. You can't know how to live like Him if you don't know what He did. That's why we included part of the gospel of John in this book so you can begin to dive into the life of Christ. As you open the Bible and learn about God, you will find God beginning to change you from the inside out. He'll show you what **NEXT** steps you need to take.

11. WHAT DO I DO WHEN I MESS UP?

We all make mistakes! We all mess up. Thank God for His grace on us. Although He has mercy on us and forgives us this should never be something we take for granted. Paul from the Bible writes about God's grace in the book of Romans. At the end of chapter 5 it talks about where sin increases grace increases. That can easily be taken out of context if you don't read the beginning of chapter 6 which says, *"What shall we say, then? Shall we go on sinning so that grace may increase? By no means! We died to sin; how can we live in it any longer?"* Some people begin to make excuses so they can stay in their life of sin. They take on the attitude that they'll just keep asking for forgiveness for the same thing again and again. They'll use the played out line, "Well, God knows my heart". Yes, he does know your heart, and He knows when you love Him and when you're just trying to play the role but it's not real. If you really experience a relationship with God and begin to fall in love with Him you'll want to please Him.

I've been married since 1996 and I love my wife with all my heart. I can honestly say we've had a great relationship that continues to get better as we grow closer together in our journey with God. We've always been faithful to each other throughout our marriage. But, if I stepped out on her with another woman and then asked for forgiveness, but then continued to do it again and again and again… eventually everyone would begin to ask me, "Do you really love her?" Because if I really love my wife, I want to please her, protect her and honor her. This shouldn't be something that someone has to constantly remind me about. If I really love her I'll have a desire to do those things and strive to make our relationship better.

In the same way if you really love God your desires will begin to change to where you want to do things that are pleasing to Him. You'll begin to see the lifestyle that is recommended for Christians in the Bible isn't a list of rules, but it's a parent looking out for His children. He's our creator, meaning He made us. He knows how we are wired. He doesn't put boundaries in place so we won't have any fun. He knows that if we sleep around with a bunch of people it will wreck us emotionally, not to mention we can physically catch a deadly disease. He knows that if we don't learn to forgive it will begin to eat us alive as we get bitter. He knows our emotions and the effects of our actions. He loves us so much and wants the best for us. There still will be times we mess up and sin. This doesn't mean we no longer have a relationship with Him. But, sin can and will bring distance between you and God.

When we mess up we need to quickly turn to God and confess it and ask for forgiveness. In the process of that we also need to repent. What does that mean? It means that you change your heart and you change your mind. It means that you literally turn from your mistakes and turn towards God and start doing it His way. So, the **NEXT** time you mess up, don't ignore it or try to hide it. Quickly deal with it and bring it to God. It's also important to have another brother or sister in Christ that you can share it with and have them pray for you and hold you accountable. James 5:16 says, *"Make this your common practice: Confess your sins to each other and pray for each other so that you can live together whole and healed." (Message)* So, be encouraged and know that God loves you and when you mess up, pick yourself back up and take these steps and move forward.

12. HOW CAN I KNOW WHAT GOD'S PURPOSE IS FOR MY LIFE? WHY AM I HERE?

This is one of the biggest questions we all have. There were several years where I was unclear what the answer was for me personally. I had dreams and things I wanted to do, but did they fit in with God's? Some did, some didn't. But, new things have come into the picture that I would have never dreamed or imagined I'd be doing. God has given all of us some unique talents and passions. The problem for all of us is figuring out what God's plan is and then how to make it happen. There is no exact formula for discovering this as God works in so many different ways. For some of us we may find this out rather quickly, while for others of us it may take a lot longer as God is trying to show us some other things along the way. Each of our journeys are different, but we should always be seeking Him about what is **NEXT**.

But, there are some things we can look at that can help us move forward in discovering God's plan for our life. We need to ask God for wisdom. Throughout the Bible it tells us that we should ask for wisdom when we don't know what to do. The New Testament book of James says, *"If you need wisdom, ask our generous God, and he will give it to you. He will not rebuke you for asking." (James 1:5 NLT)* So whatever the decision or problem, if you ask God for wisdom, He'll give it to you. He may not speak in an audible voice to you (which most of us would be terrified if He did), but you'll begin to discern in your heart what He is leading you to do. Be proactive. Don't just sit around. Have your eyes and ears open to your creator.

God uses people and circumstances to also speak to us. Those circumstances might lead you towards something you are good at. Prayerfully investigate that, do your research, try it out if you have the opportunity. You may discover this is your passion, or you may discover that it isn't for you at all. You can also ask some of your solid Christian friends about what they think God may be saying to you. Proverbs is many times called the book of wisdom. In chapter 11 verse 14 it says, *"For a lack of guidance a nation falls, but many advisers make victory sure."* Over the years I've always relied on several Godly men and women to help guide decisions in my personal life and decisions for our church.

The bottom line is that we were all created to do something in God's big plan. We must remember it's His plan... it's His movie and we all play a supporting role, but He's the star! But, the awesome thing is we get the privilege to play a part. Many of you reading this book shouldn't even be alive today, but for some reason you are still here! You know your story! God has brought you to this point to get your attention, because He wants to use you. So, go hard after His plan and put it into action!

This short book can't possibly give you every **NEXT** step, but my hope is that it gets you started on the journey. Remember, each of our journeys are going to look different as we're all called to different things. I pray that as you seek God that He'll reveal exactly what He has for you. Since I've been following Christ, my journey has been incredibly exciting with all kinds of ups, downs and surprises. Ultimately, I've learned to trust God for the future and the things unknown. I've come to watch first hand that he's in control and has my best interest in mind. We included the first 7 chapters of the book of John (aka the gospel of John) as the **NEXT** section of the book.

The book of John tells the story of Christ's life and includes His words and teachings. It was written by John who was one of the 12 disciples that Jesus chose to be part of His team throughout His ministry. I encourage you to read just one chapter over the next 3 weeks (21 days). We have the first 7 chapters here in the book, then we encourage you to transition to a physical Bible or download a Bible app and continue reading that way and move into your new rhythm of daily scripture reading.

THE BOOK OF JOHN

CHAPTERS 1 THROUGH 7

New Living Translation (NLT)

Prologue: Christ, the Eternal Word

In the beginning the Word already existed.
The Word was with God,
and the Word was God.
He existed in the beginning with God.
God created everything through him,
and nothing was created except through him.
The Word gave life to everything that was created,
and his life brought light to everyone.
The light shines in the darkness,
and the darkness can never extinguish it.

God sent a man, John the Baptist, 7 to tell about the light so that everyone might believe because of his testimony. 8 John himself was not the light; he was simply a witness to tell about the light. 9 The one who is the true light, who gives light to everyone, was coming into the world.

He came into the very world he created, but the world didn't recognize him. 11 He came to his own people, and even they rejected him. 12 But to all who believed him and accepted him, he gave the right to become children of God. 13 They are reborn—not with a physical birth resulting from human passion or plan, but a birth that comes from God.

So the Word became human and made his home among us. He was full of unfailing love and faithfulness. And we have seen his glory, the glory of the Father's one and only Son.

John testified about him when he shouted to the crowds, "This is the one I was talking about when I said, 'Someone is coming after me who is far greater than I am, for he existed long before me.'"

16 From his abundance we have all received one gracious blessing after another. 17 For the law was given through Moses, but God's unfailing love and faithfulness came through Jesus Christ. 18 No one has ever seen God. But the unique One, who is himself God, is near to the Father's heart. He has revealed God to us.

The Testimony of John the Baptist

19 This was John's testimony when the Jewish leaders sent priests and Temple assistants from Jerusalem to ask John, "Who are you?" 20 He came right out and said, "I am not the Messiah."

21 "Well then, who are you?" they asked. "Are you Elijah?"

"No," he replied.

"Are you the Prophet we are expecting?"

"No."

22 "Then who are you? We need an answer for those who sent us. What do you have to say about yourself?"

23 John replied in the words of the prophet Isaiah:

"I am a voice shouting in the wilderness,
'Clear the way for the Lord's coming!'"

24 Then the Pharisees who had been sent 25 asked him, "If you aren't the Messiah or Elijah or the Prophet, what right do you have to baptize?"

26 John told them, "I baptize with water, but right here in the crowd is someone you do not recognize. 27 Though his ministry follows mine, I'm not even worthy to be his slave and untie the straps of his sandal."

28 This encounter took place in Bethany, an area east of the Jordan River, where John was baptizing.

Jesus, the Lamb of God

29 The next day John saw Jesus coming toward him and said, "Look! The Lamb of God who takes away the sin of the world! 30 He is the one I was talking about when I said, 'A man is coming after me who is far greater than I am, for he existed long before me.' 31 I did not recognize him as the Messiah, but I have been baptizing with water so that he might be revealed to Israel."

32 Then John testified, "I saw the Holy Spirit descending like a dove from heaven and resting upon him. 33 I didn't know he was the one, but when God sent me to baptize with water, he told me, 'The one on whom you see the Spirit descend and rest is the one who will baptize with the Holy Spirit.' 34 I saw this happen to Jesus, so I testify that he is the Chosen One of God."

The First Disciples

35 The following day John was again standing with two of his disciples. 36 As Jesus walked by, John looked at him and declared, "Look! There is the Lamb of God!" 37 When John's two disciples heard this, they followed Jesus.

38 Jesus looked around and saw them following. "What do you want?" he asked them.

They replied, "Rabbi" (which means "Teacher"), "where are you staying?"

39 "Come and see," he said. It was about four o'clock in the afternoon when they went with him to the place where he was staying, and they remained with him the rest of the day.

40 Andrew, Simon Peter's brother, was one of these men who heard what John said and then followed Jesus. 41 Andrew went to find his brother, Simon, and told him, "We have found the Messiah" (which means "Christ").

42 Then Andrew brought Simon to meet Jesus. Looking intently at Simon, Jesus said, "Your name is Simon, son of John—but you will be called Cephas" (which means "Peter").

43 The next day Jesus decided to go to Galilee. He found Philip and said to him, "Come, follow me." 44 Philip was from Bethsaida, Andrew and Peter's hometown.

45 Philip went to look for Nathanael and told him "We have found the very person Moses and the prophets wrote about! His name is Jesus, the son of Joseph from Nazareth."

46 "Nazareth!" exclaimed Nathanael. "Can anything good come from Nazareth?"

"Come and see for yourself," Philip replied.

47 As they approached, Jesus said, "Now here is a genuine son of Israel—a man of complete integrity."

48 "How do you know about me?" Nathanael asked.

Jesus replied, "I could see you under the fig tree before Philip found you."

49 Then Nathanael exclaimed, "Rabbi, you are the Son of God—the King of Israel!"

50 Jesus asked him, "Do you believe this just because I told you I had seen you under the fig tree? You will see greater things than this." 51 Then he said, "I tell you the truth, you will all see heaven open and the angels of God going up and down on the Son of Man, the one who is the stairway between heaven and earth."

JOHN 2

The Wedding at Cana

2 The next day there was a wedding celebration in the village of Cana in Galilee. Jesus' mother was there, 2 and Jesus and his disciples were also invited to the celebration. 3 The wine supply ran out during the festivities, so Jesus' mother told him, "They have no more wine."

4 "Dear woman, that's not our problem," Jesus replied. "My time has not yet come."

5 But his mother told the servants, "Do whatever he tells you."

6 Standing nearby were six stone water jars, used for Jewish ceremonial washing. Each could hold twenty to thirty gallons. 7 Jesus told the servants, "Fill the jars with water." When the jars had been filled, 8 he said, "Now dip some out, and take it to the master of ceremonies." So the servants followed his instructions.

9 When the master of ceremonies tasted the water that was now wine, not knowing where it had come from (though, of course, the servants knew), he called the bridegroom over. 10 "A host always serves the best wine first," he said. "Then, when everyone has had a lot to drink, he brings out the less expensive wine. But you have kept the best until now!"

11 This miraculous sign at Cana in Galilee was the first time Jesus revealed his glory. And his disciples believed in him.

12 After the wedding he went to Capernaum for a few days with his mother, his brothers, and his disciples.

Jesus Clears the Temple

13 It was nearly time for the Jewish Passover celebration, so Jesus went to Jerusalem. 14 In the Temple area he saw merchants selling cattle, sheep, and doves for sacrifices; he also saw dealers at tables exchanging foreign money. 15 Jesus made a whip from some ropes and chased them all out of the Temple. He drove out the sheep and cattle, scattered the money changers' coins over the floor, and turned over their tables. 16 Then, going over to the people who sold doves, he told them, "Get these things out of here. Stop turning my Father's house into a marketplace!"

17 Then his disciples remembered this prophecy from the Scriptures: "Passion for God's house will consume me."

18 But the Jewish leaders demanded, "What are you doing? If God gave you authority to do this, show us a miraculous sign to prove it."

19 "All right," Jesus replied. "Destroy this temple, and in three days I will raise it up."

20 "What!" they exclaimed. "It has taken forty-six years to build this Temple, and you can rebuild it in three days?" 21 But when Jesus said "this temple," he meant his own body. 22 After he was raised from the dead, his disciples remembered he had said this, and they believed both the Scriptures and what Jesus had said.

Jesus and Nicodemus

23 Because of the miraculous signs Jesus did in Jerusalem at the Passover celebration, many began to trust in him. 24 But Jesus didn't trust them, because he knew all about people. 25 No one needed to tell him about human nature, for he knew what was in each person's heart.

JOHN 3

3 There was a man named Nicodemus, a Jewish religious leader who was a Pharisee. 2 After dark one evening, he came to speak with Jesus. "Rabbi," he said, "we all know that God has sent you to teach us. Your miraculous signs are evidence that God is with you."

3 Jesus replied, "I tell you the truth, unless you are born again, you cannot see the Kingdom of God."

4 "What do you mean?" exclaimed Nicodemus. "How can an old man go back into his mother's womb and be born again?"

5 Jesus replied, "I assure you, no one can enter the Kingdom of God without being born of water and the Spirit. 6 Humans can reproduce only human life, but the Holy Spirit gives birth to spiritual life. 7 So don't be surprised when I say, 'You must be born again.' 8 The wind blows wherever it wants. Just as you can hear the wind but can't tell where it comes from or where it is going, so you can't explain how people are born of the Spirit."

9 "How are these things possible?" Nicodemus asked.

10 Jesus replied, "You are a respected Jewish teacher, and yet you don't understand these things? 11 I assure you, we tell you what we know and have seen, and yet you won't believe our testimony. 12 But if you don't believe me when I tell you about earthly things, how can you possibly believe if I tell you about heavenly things? 13 No one has ever gone to heaven and returned. But the Son of Man has come down from heaven. 14 And as Moses lifted up the bronze snake on a pole in the wilderness, so the Son of Man must be lifted up, 15 so that everyone who believes in him will have eternal life.

16 "For this is how God loved the world: He gave his one and only Son, so that everyone who believes in him will not perish but have eternal life. 17 God sent his Son into the world not to judge the world, but to save the world through him.

18 "There is no judgment against anyone who believes in him. But anyone who does not believe in him has already been judged for not believing in God's one and only Son. 19 And the judgment

is based on this fact: God's light came into the world, but people loved the darkness more than the light, for their actions were evil. 20 All who do evil hate the light and refuse to go near it for fear their sins will be exposed. 21 But those who do what is right come to the light so others can see that they are doing what God wants."

John the Baptist Exalts Jesus

22 Then Jesus and his disciples left Jerusalem and went into the Judean countryside. Jesus spent some time with them there, baptizing people.

23 At this time John the Baptist was baptizing at Aenon, near Salim, because there was plenty of water there; and people kept coming to him for baptism. 24 (This was before John was thrown into prison.) 25 A debate broke out between John's disciples and a certain Jew over ceremonial cleansing. 26 So John's disciples came to him and said, "Rabbi, the man you met on the other side of the Jordan River, the one you identified as the Messiah, is also baptizing people. And everybody is going to him instead of coming to us."

27 John replied, "No one can receive anything unless God gives it from heaven. 28 You yourselves know how plainly I told you, 'I am not the Messiah. I am only here to prepare the way for him.' 29 It is the bridegroom who marries the bride, and the bridegroom's friend is simply glad to stand with him and hear his vows. Therefore, I am filled with joy at his success. 30 He must become greater and greater, and I must become less and less.

31 "He has come from above and is greater than anyone else. We are of the earth, and we speak of earthly things, but he has come from heaven and is greater than anyone else. 32 He testifies about what he has seen and heard, but how few believe what he tells them! 33 Anyone who accepts his testimony can affirm that God is true. 34 For he is sent by God. He speaks God's words, for God gives him the Spirit without limit. 35 The Father loves his Son and has put everything into his hands. 36 And anyone who believes in God's Son has eternal life. Anyone who doesn't obey the Son will never experience eternal life but remains under God's angry judgment."

JOHN 4

Jesus and the Samaritan Woman

4 Jesus knew the Pharisees had heard that he was baptizing and making more disciples than John 2 (though Jesus himself didn't baptize them—his disciples did). 3 So he left Judea and returned to Galilee.

4 He had to go through Samaria on the way. 5 Eventually he came to the Samaritan village of Sychar, near the field that Jacob gave to his son Joseph. 6 Jacob's well was there; and Jesus, tired from the long walk, sat wearily beside the well about noontime. 7 Soon a Samaritan woman came to draw water, and Jesus said to her, "Please give me a drink." 8 He was alone at the time because his disciples had gone into the village to buy some food.

9 The woman was surprised, for Jews refuse to have anything to do with Samaritans. She said to Jesus, "You are a Jew, and I am a Samaritan woman. Why are you asking me for a drink?"

10 Jesus replied, "If you only knew the gift God has for you and who you are speaking to, you would ask me, and I would give you living water."

11 "But sir, you don't have a rope or a bucket," she said, "and this well is very deep. Where would you get this living water? 12 And besides, do you think you're greater than our ancestor Jacob, who gave us this well? How can you offer better water than he and his sons and his animals enjoyed?"

13 Jesus replied, "Anyone who drinks this water will soon become thirsty again. 14 But those who drink the water I give will never be thirsty again. It becomes a fresh, bubbling spring within them, giving them eternal life."

15 "Please, sir," the woman said, "give me this water! Then I'll never be thirsty again, and I won't have to come here to get water."

16 "Go and get your husband," Jesus told her.

17 "I don't have a husband," the woman replied.

Jesus said, "You're right! You don't have a husband— 18 for you have had five husbands, and you aren't even married to the man you're living with now. You certainly spoke the truth!"

19 "Sir," the woman said, "you must be a prophet. 20 So tell me, why is it that you Jews insist that Jerusalem is the only place of worship, while we Samaritans claim it is here at Mount Gerizim, where our ancestors worshiped?"

21 Jesus replied, "Believe me, dear woman, the time is coming when it will no longer matter whether you worship the Father on this mountain or in Jerusalem. 22 You Samaritans know very little about the one you worship, while we Jews know all about him, for salvation comes through the Jews. 23 But the time is coming— indeed it's here now—when true worshipers will worship the Father in spirit and in truth. The Father is looking for those who will worship him that way. 24 For God is Spirit, so those who worship him must worship in spirit and in truth."

25 The woman said, "I know the Messiah is coming—the one who is called Christ. When he comes, he will explain everything to us."

26 Then Jesus told her, "I am the Messiah!"

27 Just then his disciples came back. They were shocked to find him talking to a woman, but none of them had the nerve to ask, "What do you want with her?" or "Why are you talking to her?" 28 The woman left her water jar beside the well and ran back to the village, telling everyone, 29 "Come and see a man who told me everything I ever did! Could he possibly be the Messiah?" 30 So the people came streaming from the village to see him.

31 Meanwhile, the disciples were urging Jesus, "Rabbi, eat something."

32 But Jesus replied, "I have a kind of food you know nothing about."

33 "Did someone bring him food while we were gone?" the disciples asked each other.

34 Then Jesus explained: "My nourishment comes from doing the will of God, who sent me, and from finishing his work. 35 You know the saying, 'Four months between planting and harvest.' But I say, wake up and look around. The fields are already ripe for harvest. 36 The harvesters are paid good wages, and the fruit they harvest is people brought to eternal life. What joy awaits both the planter and the harvester alike! 37 You know the saying, 'One plants and another harvests.' And it's true. 38 I sent you to harvest where you didn't plant; others had already done the work, and now you will get to gather the harvest."

Many Samaritans Believe

39 Many Samaritans from the village believed in Jesus because the woman had said, "He told me everything I ever did!" 40 When they came out to see him, they begged him to stay in their village. So he stayed for two days, 41 long enough for many more to hear his message and believe. 42 Then they said to the woman, "Now we believe, not just because of what you told us, but because we have heard him ourselves. Now we know that he is indeed the Savior of the world."

Jesus Heals an Official's Son

43 At the end of the two days, Jesus went on to Galilee. 44 He himself had said that a prophet is not honored in his own hometown. 45 Yet the Galileans welcomed him, for they had been in Jerusalem at the Passover celebration and had seen everything he did there.

46 As he traveled through Galilee, he came to Cana, where he had turned the water into wine. There was a government official in nearby Capernaum whose son was very sick. 47 When he heard that Jesus had come from Judea to Galilee, he went and begged Jesus to come to Capernaum to heal his son, who was about to die.

48 Jesus asked, "Will you never believe in me unless you see miraculous signs and wonders?"

49 The official pleaded, "Lord, please come now before my little boy dies."

50 Then Jesus told him, "Go back home. Your son will live!" And the man believed what Jesus said and started home.

51 While the man was on his way, some of his servants met him with the news that his son was alive and well. 52 He asked them when the boy had begun to get better, and they replied, "Yesterday afternoon at one o'clock his fever suddenly disappeared!" 53 Then the father realized that that was the very time Jesus had told him, "Your son will live." And he and his entire household believed in Jesus. 54 This was the second miraculous sign Jesus did in Galilee after coming from Judea.

Jesus Heals a Lame Man

5 Afterward Jesus returned to Jerusalem for one of the Jewish holy days. 2 Inside the city, near the Sheep Gate, was the pool of Bethesda, with five covered porches. 3 Crowds of sick people—blind, lame, or paralyzed—lay on the porches. 5 One of the men lying there had been sick for thirty-eight years. 6 When Jesus saw him and knew he had been ill for a long time, he asked him, "Would you like to get well?"

7 "I can't, sir," the sick man said, "for I have no one to put me into the pool when the water bubbles up. Someone else always gets there ahead of me."

8 Jesus told him, "Stand up, pick up your mat, and walk!"

9 Instantly, the man was healed! He rolled up his sleeping mat and began walking! But this miracle happened on the Sabbath, 10 so the Jewish leaders objected. They said to the man who was cured, "You can't work on the Sabbath! The law doesn't allow you to carry that sleeping mat!"

11 But he replied, "The man who healed me told me, 'Pick up your mat and walk.'"

12 "Who said such a thing as that?" they demanded.

13 The man didn't know, for Jesus had disappeared into the crowd. 14 But afterward Jesus found him in the Temple and told him, "Now you are well; so stop sinning, or something even worse may happen to you." 15 Then the man went and told the Jewish leaders that it was Jesus who had healed him.

Jesus Claims to Be the Son of God

16 So the Jewish leaders began harassing Jesus for breaking the Sabbath rules. 17 But Jesus replied, "My Father is always working, and so am I." 18 So the Jewish leaders tried all the harder to find a way to kill him. For he not only broke the Sabbath, he called God his Father, thereby making himself equal with God.

19 So Jesus explained, "I tell you the truth, the Son can do nothing by himself. He does only what he sees the Father doing. Whatever the Father does, the Son also does. 20 For the Father loves the Son and shows him everything he is doing. In fact, the Father will show him how to do even greater works than healing this man. Then you will truly be astonished. 21 For just as the Father gives life to those he raises from the dead, so the Son gives life to anyone he wants. 22 In addition, the Father judges no one. Instead, he has given the Son absolute authority to judge, 23 so that everyone will honor the Son, just as they honor the Father. Anyone who does not honor the Son is certainly not honoring the Father who sent him.

24 "I tell you the truth, those who listen to my message and believe in God who sent me have eternal life. They will never be condemned for their sins, but they have already passed from death into life.

25 "And I assure you that the time is coming, indeed it's here now, when the dead will hear my voice—the voice of the Son of God. And

those who listen will live. 26 The Father has life in himself, and he has granted that same life-giving power to his Son. 27 And he has given him authority to judge everyone because he is the Son of Man. 28 Don't be so surprised! Indeed, the time is coming when all the dead in their graves will hear the voice of God's Son, 29 and they will rise again. Those who have done good will rise to experience eternal life, and those who have continued in evil will rise to experience judgment. 30 I can do nothing on my own. I judge as God tells me. Therefore, my judgment is just, because I carry out the will of the one who sent me, not my own will.

Witnesses to Jesus

31 "If I were to testify on my own behalf, my testimony would not be valid. 32 But someone else is also testifying about me, and I assure you that everything he says about me is true. 33 In fact, you sent investigators to listen to John the Baptist, and his testimony about me was true. 34 Of course, I have no need of human witnesses, but I say these things so you might be saved. 35 John was like a burning and shining lamp, and you were excited for a while about his message. 36 But I have a greater witness than John—my teachings and my miracles. The Father gave me these works to accomplish, and they prove that he sent me. 37 And the Father who sent me has testified about me himself. You have never heard his voice or seen him face to face, 38 and you do not have his message in your hearts, because you do not believe me—the one he sent to you.

39 "You search the Scriptures because you think they give you eternal life. But the Scriptures point to me! 40 Yet you refuse to come to me to receive this life.

41 "Your approval means nothing to me, 42 because I know you don't have God's love within you. 43 For I have come to you in my Father's name, and you have rejected me. Yet if others come in their own name, you gladly welcome them. 44 No wonder you can't believe! For you gladly honor each other, but you don't care about the honor that comes from the one who alone is God.

45 "Yet it isn't I who will accuse you before the Father. Moses will accuse you! Yes, Moses, in whom you put your hopes. 46 If you really believed Moses, you would believe me, because he wrote about me. 47 But since you don't believe what he wrote, how will you believe what I say?"

JOHN 6

Jesus Feeds Five Thousand

6 After this, Jesus crossed over to the far side of the Sea of Galilee, also known as the Sea of Tiberias. 2 A huge crowd kept following him wherever he went, because they saw his miraculous signs as he healed the sick. 3 Then Jesus climbed a hill and sat down with his disciples around him. 4 (It was nearly time for the Jewish Passover celebration.) 5 Jesus soon saw a huge crowd of people coming to look for him. Turning to Philip, he asked, "Where can we buy bread to feed all these people?" 6 He was testing Philip, for he already knew what he was going to do.

7 Philip replied, "Even if we worked for months, we wouldn't have enough money to feed them!"

8 Then Andrew, Simon Peter's brother, spoke up. 9 "There's a young boy here with five barley loaves and two fish. But what good is that with this huge crowd?"

10 "Tell everyone to sit down," Jesus said. So they all sat down on the grassy slopes. (The men alone numbered about 5,000.) 11 Then Jesus took the loaves, gave thanks to God, and distributed them to the people. Afterward he did the same with the fish. And they all ate as much as they wanted. 12 After everyone was full, Jesus told his disciples, "Now gather the leftovers, so that nothing is wasted." 13 So they picked up the pieces and filled twelve baskets with scraps left by the people who had eaten from the five barley loaves.

14 When the people saw him do this miraculous sign, they exclaimed, "Surely, he is the Prophet we have been expecting!" 15 When Jesus saw that they were ready to force him to be their king, he slipped away into the hills by himself.

Jesus Walks on Water

16 That evening Jesus' disciples went down to the shore to wait for him. 17 But as darkness fell and Jesus still hadn't come back, they got into the boat and headed across the lake toward Capernaum. 18 Soon a gale swept down upon them, and the sea grew very rough. 19 They had rowed three or four miles when suddenly they saw Jesus walking on the water toward the boat. They were terrified, 20 but he called out to them, "Don't be afraid. I am here!" 21 Then

they were eager to let him in the boat, and immediately they arrived at their destination!

Jesus, the Bread of Life

22 The next day the crowd that had stayed on the far shore saw that the disciples had taken the only boat, and they realized Jesus had not gone with them. 23 Several boats from Tiberias landed near the place where the Lord had blessed the bread and the people had eaten. 24 So when the crowd saw that neither Jesus nor his disciples were there, they got into the boats and went across to Capernaum to look for him. 25 They found him on the other side of the lake and asked, "Rabbi, when did you get here?"

26 Jesus replied, "I tell you the truth, you want to be with me because I fed you, not because you understood the miraculous signs. 27 But don't be so concerned about perishable things like food. Spend your energy seeking the eternal life that the Son of Man can give you. For God the Father has given me the seal of his approval."

28 They replied, "We want to perform God's works, too. What should we do?"

29 Jesus told them, "This is the only work God wants from you: Believe in the one he has sent."

30 They answered, "Show us a miraculous sign if you want us to believe in you. What can you do? 31 After all, our ancestors ate manna while they journeyed through the wilderness! The Scriptures say, 'Moses gave them bread from heaven to eat.'"

32 Jesus said, "I tell you the truth, Moses didn't

ive you bread from heaven. My Father did.
nd now he offers you the true bread from
eaven. 33 The true bread of God is the one who
omes down from heaven and gives life to the
orld."

4 "Sir," they said, "give us that bread every day."

5 Jesus replied, "I am the bread of life.
Vhoever comes to me will never be hungry
gain. Whoever believes in me will never be
irsty. 36 But you haven't believed in me even
ough you have seen me. 37 However, those
e Father has given me will come to me, and I
ill never reject them. 38 For I have come down
om heaven to do the will of God who sent me,
ot to do my own will. 39 And this is the will of
od, that I should not lose even one of all those
e has given me, but that I should raise them up
t the last day. 40 For it is my Father's will that all
ho see his Son and believe in him should have
ternal life. I will raise them up at the last day."

Then the people began to murmur in
isagreement because he had said, "I am the
read that came down from heaven." 42 They
id, "Isn't this Jesus, the son of Joseph? We
ow his father and mother. How can he say, 'I
me down from heaven'?"

But Jesus replied, "Stop complaining about
hat I said. 44 For no one can come to me unless
e Father who sent me draws them to me, and
the last day I will raise them up. 45 As it is
ritten in the Scriptures, 'They will all be taught
God.' Everyone who listens to the Father and
arns from him comes to me. 46 (Not that anyone
as ever seen the Father; only I, who was sent
om God, have seen him.)

47 "I tell you the truth, anyone who believes has
eternal life. 48 Yes, I am the bread of life! 49 Your
ancestors ate manna in the wilderness, but they
all died. 50 Anyone who eats the bread from
heaven, however, will never die. 51 I am the living
bread that came down from heaven. Anyone who
eats this bread will live forever; and this bread,
which I will offer so the world may live, is my
flesh."

52 Then the people began arguing with each
other about what he meant. "How can this man
give us his flesh to eat?" they asked.

53 So Jesus said again, "I tell you the truth, unless
you eat the flesh of the Son of Man and drink
his blood, you cannot have eternal life within
you. 54 But anyone who eats my flesh and drinks
my blood has eternal life, and I will raise that
person at the last day. 55 For my flesh is true food,
and my blood is true drink. 56 Anyone who eats
my flesh and drinks my blood remains in me, and
I in him. 57 I live because of the living Father who
sent me; in the same way, anyone who feeds
on me will live because of me. 58 I am the true
bread that came down from heaven. Anyone who
eats this bread will not die as your ancestors did
(even though they ate the manna) but will live
forever."

59 He said these things while he was teaching in
the synagogue in Capernaum.

Many Disciples Desert Jesus

60 Many of his disciples said, "This is very hard to
understand. How can anyone accept it?"

61 Jesus was aware that his disciples were complaining, so he said to them, "Does this offend you? 62 Then what will you think if you see the Son of Man ascend to heaven again? 63 The Spirit alone gives eternal life. Human effort accomplishes nothing. And the very words I have spoken to you are spirit and life. 64 But some of you do not believe me." (For Jesus knew from the beginning which ones didn't believe, and he knew who would betray him.) 65 Then he said, "That is why I said that people can't come to me unless the Father gives them to me."

66 At this point many of his disciples turned away and deserted him. 67 Then Jesus turned to the Twelve and asked, "Are you also going to leave?"

68 Simon Peter replied, "Lord, to whom would we go? You have the words that give eternal life. 69 We believe, and we know you are the Holy One of God."

70 Then Jesus said, "I chose the twelve of you, but one is a devil." 71 He was speaking of Judas, son of Simon Iscariot, one of the Twelve, who would later betray him.

JOHN 7

Jesus and His Brothers

7 After this, Jesus traveled around Galilee. He wanted to stay out of Judea, where the Jewish leaders were plotting his death. 2 But soon it was time for the Jewish Festival of Shelters, 3 and Jesus' brothers said to him, "Leave here and go to Judea, where your followers can see your miracles! 4 You can't become famous if you hide like this! If you can do such wonderful things, show yourself to the world!" 5 For even his brothers didn't believe in him.

6 Jesus replied, "Now is not the right time for me to go, but you can go anytime. 7 The world can't hate you, but it does hate me because I accuse it of doing evil. 8 You go on. I'm not going to this festival, because my time has not yet come." 9 After saying these things, Jesus remained in Galilee.

Jesus Teaches Openly at the Temple

10 But after his brothers left for the festival, Jesus also went, though secretly, staying out of public view. 11 The Jewish leaders tried to find him at the festival and kept asking if anyone had seen him. 12 There was a lot of grumbling about him among the crowds. Some argued, "He's a good man," but others said, "He's nothing but a fraud who deceives the people." 13 But no one had the courage to speak favorably about him in public, for they were afraid of getting in trouble with the Jewish leaders.

14 Then, midway through the festival, Jesus went up to the Temple and began to teach. 15 The people were surprised when they heard him. "How does he know so much when he hasn't been trained?" they asked.

16 So Jesus told them, "My message is not my own; it comes from God who sent me. 17 Anyone who wants to do the will of God will know whether my teaching is from God or is merely my own. 18 Those who speak for themselves want glory only for themselves, but a person who seeks to honor the one who sent him speaks truth, not lies. 19 Moses gave you the law, but

one of you obeys it! In fact, you are trying to kill me."

The crowd replied, "You're demon possessed! Who's trying to kill you?"

Jesus replied, "I did one miracle on the Sabbath, and you were amazed. 22 But you work on the Sabbath, too, when you obey Moses' law of circumcision. (Actually, this tradition of circumcision began with the patriarchs, long before the law of Moses.) 23 For if the correct time for circumcising your son falls on the Sabbath, you go ahead and do it so as not to break the law of Moses. So why should you be angry with me for healing a man on the Sabbath? 24 Look beneath the surface so you can judge correctly."

Jesus the Messiah?

Some of the people who lived in Jerusalem started to ask each other, "Isn't this the man they are trying to kill? 26 But here he is, speaking in public, and they say nothing to him. Could our leaders possibly believe that he is the Messiah? 27 But how could he be? For we know where this man comes from. When the Messiah comes, he will simply appear; no one will know where he comes from."

While Jesus was teaching in the Temple, he called out, "Yes, you know me, and you know where I come from. But I'm not here on my own. The one who sent me is true, and you don't know him. 29 But I know him because I come from him, and he sent me to you." 30 Then the leaders tried to arrest him; but no one laid a hand on him, because his time had not yet come.

31 Many among the crowds at the Temple believed in him. "After all," they said, "would you expect the Messiah to do more miraculous signs than this man has done?"

32 When the Pharisees heard that the crowds were whispering such things, they and the leading priests sent Temple guards to arrest Jesus. 33 But Jesus told them, "I will be with you only a little longer. Then I will return to the one who sent me. 34 You will search for me but not find me. And you cannot go where I am going."

35 The Jewish leaders were puzzled by this statement. "Where is he planning to go?" they asked. "Is he thinking of leaving the country and going to the Jews in other lands? Maybe he will even teach the Greeks! 36 What does he mean when he says, 'You will search for me but not find me,' and 'You cannot go where I am going'?"

Jesus Promises Living Water

37 On the last day, the climax of the festival, Jesus stood and shouted to the crowds, "Anyone who is thirsty may come to me! 38 Anyone who believes in me may come and drink! For the Scriptures declare, 'Rivers of living water will flow from his heart.'" 39 (When he said "living water," he was speaking of the Spirit, who would be given to everyone believing in him. But the Spirit had not yet been given, because Jesus had not yet entered into his glory.)

Division and Unbelief

40 When the crowds heard him say this, some of them declared, "Surely this man is the Prophet we've been expecting." 41 Others said, "He is the Messiah." Still others said, "But he can't be! Will the Messiah come from Galilee? 42 For the Scriptures clearly state that the Messiah will be born of the royal line of David, in Bethlehem, the village where King David was born." 43 So the crowd was divided about him. 44 Some even wanted him arrested, but no one laid a hand on him.

45 When the Temple guards returned without having arrested Jesus, the leading priests and Pharisees demanded, "Why didn't you bring him in?"

46 "We have never heard anyone speak like this!" the guards responded.

47 "Have you been led astray, too?" the Pharisees mocked. 48 "Is there a single one of us rulers or Pharisees who believes in him? 49 This foolish crowd follows him, but they are ignorant of the law. God's curse is on them!"

50 Then Nicodemus, the leader who had met with Jesus earlier, spoke up. 51 "Is it legal to convict a man before he is given a hearing?" he asked.

52 They replied, "Are you from Galilee, too? Search the Scriptures and see for yourself—no prophet ever comes from Galilee!"

[The most ancient Greek manuscripts do not include John 7:53–8:11.]

53 Then the meeting broke up, and everybody went home.

New Living Translation (NLT)

Holy Bible, New Living Translation, copyright © 1996, 2004 2015 by Tyndale House Foundation. Used by permission of Tyndale House Publishers, Inc., Carol Stream, Illinois 60188 All rights reserved.

Tommy "Urban D." Kyllonen was raised in the Philadelphia area. He strayed from God as a teen, but got reconnected with his creator and followed a calling into urban ministry. In 1996 he graduated from Southeastern University with a BA in Pastoral Theology and a concentration in Youth Ministry. In 2006 he completed a master's level church leadership cohort at Southeastern University. Tommy is a creative innovator that wears many hats and always strives for what God has **NEXT**

He has been in full time ministry at Crossover Church since 1996. The first six years he served as the youth pastor and since 2002 he has served as the lead pastor. Tommy is also a hip-hop recording artist (Urban D.) that has released 9 full albums. As a speaker and artist he has ministered at over 1,000 venues in the US, Germany, Japan, UK, Australia and Africa. Tommy's passion is evident from speaking in the general session at Rick Warren's Purpose Driven Conference in California to rocking a set in an arena to performing at Riker's Island Prison in New York City. God is using him to reach a group of people that are generally elusive to the conventional church.

In addition to pastor and artist he is also a writer. He has written for Relevant, Thomas Nelson, American Bible Society, UYWI and several other publications. Tommy is the publisher of S.O.U.LMAG magazine which has become Christian hip-hop's voice in print with 28 issues produced. In addition to the NEXT book, he also wrote Un.orthodox, ReBuild and Love Our City. Whether he is speaking, rapping or writing he uses these mediums as a canvas to paint the picture of how his story has been transformed by God's story. All this could never be done without the incredible support, love and prayer from his best friend and partner Lucy. Together they raise their daughters Deyana and Sophia in Tampa, Florida.

You can learn more about Pastor Tommy at

www.**urband**.org

follow "Urband813" on all social platforms

Walking our **NEXT** steps at Crossover Church.

Pastor Tommy & Lucy Kyllonen

Hip-Hop Pioneer; Christopher "Play" Martin (from Kid n' Play) getting baptized

Crossover was started in the early 90's to reach people in the urban community that weren't going to the traditional church. In 1996 Pastor Joe McCutchen brought in Tommy Kyllonen to start the youth ministry. Over the next six years a new model of urban youth ministry was birthed that reached hundreds of unchurched teens and young adults. In 2002 the church was relaunched with new vision and structure as Tommy became the lead pastor. Crossover carefully and prayerfully began to make several changes to better reach the community. The service grew quickly as several new people came and built relationships with Christ. They began getting discipled and then got plugged in to serving others. Due to the growth and limited space, a second service was started and then eventually a third service.

God has called Crossover to be a pioneering church in reaching those influenced by Urban/ Hip-Hop Culture. Because of the church's unique approach they have been featured in USA Today, Newsweek, CBS News and several local media outlets. Outreach Magazine listed them as one of America's Most Innovative Churches. As many around the world began to look at Crossover as a model they launched an annual leadership conference "Flavor Fest" to equip leaders to better reach the culture. Over 5,000 leaders have been trained at the conference over the years. Numerous CD's, books, magazines and resources have been produced by Pastor Tommy and other innovators at the church.

Their former North Orleans campus was completely renovated and transformed into a place exploding with creativity. At that location the church grew from 40 to over 500 that attended 3 Sunday Services. Although the North Orleans campus was a cool space, it was maxed out. Pastor Tommy and the leadership team prayed about the next steps and even in the middle of a recession they along with the membership decided to put the campus up for sale in late 2008. In January of 2010 the campus was sold to a Haitian Church and Crossover became a portable church meeting at a hotel. They experienced a season of more growth and miracles at the hotel. During this time they signed a deal on a former Toys R' Us retail building. In the Fall of 2010 they moved into their newly remodeled 43,000 square foot building on Fowler Ave. Since then they have been able to reach the city in multiple new ways as they have seen thousands start a new relationship with Christ and over 1,400 people get baptized. In 2019 they nationally launched their Love Our City campaign to equip churches to reach thousands of new people in their communities. Hundreds of churches have joined the growing Love Our City movement. The church also launched their new location in the city of Atlanta in 2019 - Crossover Church ATL! We can't wait to see what's **NEXT**!

Pastor Tommy praying over Montell Jordan

DISCOVER · DEVELOP · DISPLAY

www.crossoverchurch.org

follow us on all social platforms "Crossover813"

EVERYTHING YOUR CHURCH OR ORGANIZATION NEEDS
TO REACH THOUSANDS OF NEW PEOPLE IN YOUR COMMUNITY!

JOIN HUNDREDS OF CHURCHES IN THE LOVE OUR CITY MOVEMENT AS THE LEADERS KIT INCLUDES A THUMB DRIVE WITH A MESSAGE SERIES, SMALL GROUP VIDEO CURRICULUM, ARTWORK, VIDEOS, PROJECT TEMPLATES, THE NEW LOVE OUR CITY HIP-HOP CD AND MORE. PLUS, THE LEADERS GUIDE GIVES YOU THE NUTS AND BOLTS ON HOW TO GET CORPORATE SPONSORS AND RAISE UP AN ARMY OF VOLUNTEERS TO SERVE THOUSANDS.

AVAILABLE EXCLUSIVELY AT
www.LOVEOURCITYBOOK.com

"ETERNAL"

clothing

NEXT

STEPS ON YOUR SPIRITUAL JOURNEY

TOMMY "URBAN D." KYLLONEN

Tranzlation Leadership
TAMPA, FLORIDA